IN EVERY BITE OF NOURISHMENT
A SEED OF WELLNESS GROWS
CULTIVATING TRANSFORMATION
WHERE HEALING FREELY FLOWS

M.C.Bell.

In the wake of losing my niece, an integral part of our family business and my daily life, I was lost in survivor's guilt and emotional turmoil. At 74, my successful business career had not prepared me for the depth of this loss. The accident left me navigating grief and a whirlwind of unresolved feelings, including intense rage and sadness.

Then, I encountered Michele. She ushered me into a space of grace and dignity, revealing a path of connection I hadn't known was possible. Guiding me through techniques to combat depression, reduce stress, and fully embrace the present, she made prayer, meditation, and conscious breathing part of my daily practice. Her 30-day challenges and the holistic support she offered, spanning from personal loss to business insights, catalyzed a transformative journey.

Michele's impact didn't stop with emotional healing. She introduced me to her eating healthy modality—incorporating balanced diets, regular exercise, and supplements into my daily regimen. These changes, under her guidance, not only improved my mental clarity but also led to significant weight loss and helped me stop drinking. Michele's approach broke me down and rebuilt me, a process my family witnessed as I underwent these massive shifts.

Michele led me to a profound state of gratitude. Encouraging me to write letters and share my innermost thoughts in a safe, authentic environment fostered a healing I hadn't imagined.

She rekindled joy in my life, showing me that profound transformation is attainable at any age. Her expertise and genuine presence revitalized me, giving me back to myself healthier and more vibrant.

Through Michele, I discovered the power of connection, skillfully threading my story into the broader mosaic of life and connection.

– MICHAEL W. HUMPHREY

Foundation of
EMBRACE

Prelude to 7th Stage

This foundational section provides a comprehensive overview of *The 7 Stages of Grief*, setting the stage for the deep dive into **EAT HEALTHY** that follows. While it serves as an introduction, it is designed to be revisited, offering insight and context as you navigate through each stage of your journey.

The EMBRACE Journey
Transform Grief and
Discover Inner *Strength*

Welcome, Warriors, to the extraordinary dimension of the 7 Stages of Grief Workbook Journal. I will guide you through a miraculous and empowering passage, unveiling the hidden treasures amidst the labyrinth of trauma and loss.

This course was born from my authentic desire to *heal it forward* in the grief community, ignited by theta meditation and a deep desire to manifest growth and healing through my writings. Drawing upon my intuitive theta-visions, I have created the EMBRACE framework — a radiant constellation of seven stages illuminating our transformative expedition in the wake of adversity.

In contrast to conventional approaches that merely skim the surface of emotions within the limited confines of the five stages of grief, I sensed the dire need for a holistic and transformative tapestry. The 7 stages of grief, meticulously crafted through my Healing it Forward modalities used in my 1:1 sacred retreats, transcend the ephemeral realm of emotions, ushering us into a realm where storytelling, the sacred utterance of our beloved's name, and the cultivation of gratitude mingle, guiding us through each challenging obstacle that graces our path.

Within this cherished community of kindred souls, we will unite, bound by a shared mission to collaborate, share our truth, and breathe life into one another's spirits—a sacred alchemy that fosters a radiant cascade of healing and metamorphosis. The modalities unveiled in the EMBRACE workbook journal's resplendent pages revolutionized how we navigate our sacred inner landscape, transforming the lives of those who have an unwavering longing to embrace the transformative work ahead.

As an extraordinary boon, I invite you to journey beside me as a Certified Grief Wellness Warrior, armed with the profound and purposeful modalities needed to extend a gentle hand to those ensnared in the clutches of their grief. By immersing yourself in these transformative practices and obtaining certification, you shall illuminate the path for others in their darkest moments, serving as a beacon of light and hope amidst the unfathomable abyss.

With deepest gratitude and genuine admiration, I extend my heartfelt appreciation to you for summoning the courage to embark upon the sacred journey of the EMBRACE workbook journal course. I assure you, Warriors, that this decision shall cascade with blessings and profoundly resonate. Together, let us traverse the infinite depths of grief, unlocking the wellspring of our inner fortitude and embarking upon a journey that transcends healing alone—a voyage brimming with purpose, renewal, and the willful power of the human spirit.

Prepare yourself for the transformational power of the 7 Stages of Grief Workbook Journal.

Let our extraordinary odyssey begin.

The Grief Warrior

Table of Contents

FOREWARD

My name is Cristal Sampson, and I work in mental health and psychiatry as a nurse practitioner in the UK, Connecticut, and New York, specializing in traumatic stress and mood disorders. I am also a young woman who experienced an early-term spontaneous miscarriage that burned a hole in depths I had previously not known existed. The revelation of this new depth of unconditional love, coupled with my baby's teeny heart stopping, left me hollow.

Even in my subsequent pregnancy the following year, I still felt empty of the unfulfillable desire for the baby back that I had lost in this life. The emptiness was filled with sadness, anxiety, and disappointment from troubled family dynamics – *a family unaware of my loss and grief.*

Someone with my expertise is never immune to the heartaches of the human experience, such as the loss of love and life. I recognized the potential to become an emotionally absent mother to my unborn baby, a fate that seemed all but certain at the time – and the thought terrified me. I am grateful to have understood that both my baby and I deserved the opportunity to heal. In my research, I discovered Michele, The Grief Warrior®.

As a health professional and a mental health specialist, I am particularly discerning about the services I opt for and the providers I choose. During this chapter of my life and given the circumstances, I did not pursue "traditional" mental health counseling. At that moment, confronting the challenges presented by contemporary therapy seemed beyond my capacity. I perceived the potential for a more conventional approach to be beneficial later in my healing journey.

What Michele provided touched the very core, breadth, and depth of my pain, reaching deep into the spiritual, mental, emotional, and energetic aspects of my being, body, and environment through a one-on-one retreat. I have not encountered anything like it since. Therefore, I am deeply moved that you are here, exploring the 7 Stages of Grief. Your journey with Michele's intentional energy, as conveyed through her books, and her custom human design modalities coupled with her healing energy, will extensively shift your essence and transform you.

FOREWARD

The '*EMBRACE: The 7 Stages of Grief*' workbook series is designed to support every individual navigating grief—those who feel unprepared and overwhelmed by the complexities of losing a loved one. This series speaks to the heart of those oscillating between the anticipation of loss and the necessity of maintaining 'normalcy,' amidst the swirl of anger, resentment, and sorrow. It is a compassionate companion for every silent sufferer, for those caught in the emotional storm of impending loss, and for caregivers in dire need of nurturing themselves.

What distinguishes Michele's '*The 7 Stages of Grief*' series most is the infusion of practical hope within its pages—a hope that is both tangible and deeply rooted in the natural spaces where resilience and healing begin. Michele brings a deep understanding and mastery in guiding others through the vast resources available for grief support, offering pathways that are both practical and easily navigable. Her insight into the caregiver journey, as a single mother is profoundly intimate, shaped by her own experience of lovingly supporting her teenage son, through his transition, enveloped in a cocoon of love. This unique perspective enriches her approach, making her guidance not only informed but deeply empathetic to the nuanced experiences of grief.

My work with Michele has caused a seismic shift in my perspective and has improved my relationships with myself, my family, and the people who meet me. I am moved with infinite gratitude at the positive and priceless impact my work with Michele has had on my experience of motherhood and the beautiful relationship my daughter and I get to have. Now, I enjoy expanding my connection as she has become a selfless friend and true mentor.

I encourage you to allow this book to transform you positively. Let it be a daily source of support and comfort, especially in moments of need. Remember, everything Michele has undertaken since Nicky's return to the Source has been a heartfelt ode to him and a homage to the enduring legacy of love and purpose he entrusted to her. Michele's ultimate wish is for you to discover your purpose and allow it to drive you forward through the cherished journey of your life.

Cristal Sampson

FROM MY HEART
to yours...

Alignment in the face of loss is the only option. When we open ourselves to the possibilities presented to us, we find this harmony: in the strength of our words, in the peace of our meditations, in the gift of our presence, in the renewal of our bodies, in the stirring of our spirits, in the depth of our relationships, and in the nourishment we give ourselves.

The path to recovery is a beautiful tapestry that offers the opportunity for personal development and the forging of inner fortitude. We will brave new territory together, learn new things, and grow as people. I will be your guide and source of solace throughout our journey together. Get ready to reclaim your life with renewed confidence as you learn to swiftly navigate life's complications and unleash your remarkable inner potential.

There is nothing scary or complicated about this course since I will be there to guide you through every one of the steps. Let's take off on a journey into the unknown, where the payoff to SELF could be infinite.

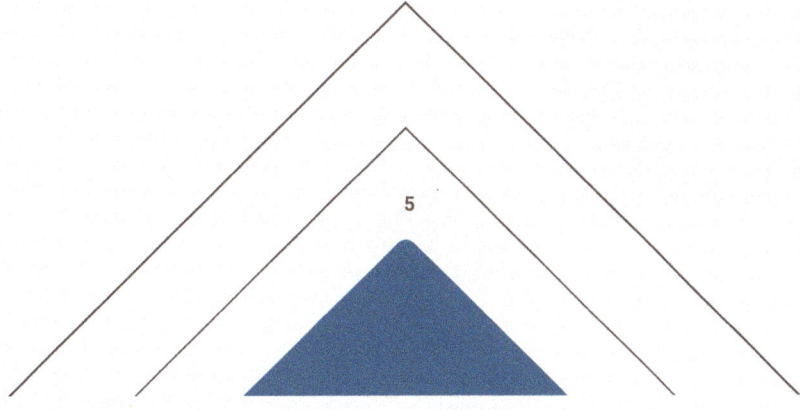

PROLONGED
GRIEF DISORDER
Unveiled
as total B.S

Shattering the Illusion: Liberating Ourselves from the Constraints of the "5 Stages of Grief"

Adhering to established norms is a delusion, a fallacy we must quickly let go of when dealing with extended grief disorder. The "5 Stages of Bereavement" model developed by psychologists has been widely disseminated for too long, permeating every aspect of grief counseling and education.

Unfortunately, the constant push to conform to a set and narrow path of grieving has led me and countless other seekers within the grief community to feel disillusioned.

I beg you to disregard this erroneous advice immediately. The core meaning of our name, "EMBRACE," contains the whole truth. The concept of "Prolonged Grief Disorder" is 100% bogus.

The "5 Stages of Grief" concept originated from an unsupported theory meant to characterize the reaction of people who had been given fatal diagnoses rather than those who were navigating the maze of loss and sorrow. Here we have two utterly dissimilar yet actual experiences, each of which calls for special attention and comprehension.

UNVEILING THE TRUTH

The Evolution from 5 Stages of Grief to Prolonged Grief Disorder

In March 2022, a new grief-related disorder was officially adopted into mainstream mental health diagnosis nomenclature. Seeing how the clinical world has further shamed the sacred grieving world is disheartening. DSM-5's trauma and stress-related category have a new label: Prolonged Grief Disorder, created deliberately to define what grief should and should not look like.

But first, let's take a moment to think. What exactly is this thing called "Prolonged Grief Disorder"? Claiming a year for adults and a paltry six months for children is an arrogant attempt to restrict the complex fabric of grief inside the confines of time. According to the American Psychological Association, persons who carry this label are assumed to exhibit the following symptoms even after the diagnostic window has closed:

- The crushing weight of grief pressed down on every aspect of their being.
- An unending fixation on sorrow as memories of the lost reverberate ceaselessly.
- A mental panorama obscured by agony or the unsettling absence of feeling.
- They engage in a delicate dance of denial and avoidance as they try to face their loved one's death.
- Dissonance and disconnection can develop when one feels different from the social norm.
- Every breath is filled with the haunting repercussions of despair and isolation.

We stand at the intersection of societal, cultural, and religious expectations, where the mere fulfillment of established criteria has become pivotal in making a prognosis. Understandably, when engulfed by the darkness of losing a loved one, such clinical classifications may not bring the peace and comprehension one wants.

To promote genuine healing, we need to permit ourselves to explore our inner emotional landscape freely.

Let us stand up as one in our resolve to overcome this stereotype's obstacles. Let us regain our freedom from societal norms to grieve and heal as we see fit.

We will overcome obstacles as a group and EMBRACE the journey of getting to the heart of our pain and reclaiming our ways forward in healing.

WHY PROLONGED GRIEF DISORDER
is Facing So Much Criticism

There is no moral compass in the arena of mourning.

Grief isn't reducible to a single feeling but incorporates many of them. It weaves a complex and ever-changing mosaic of emotions, including sadness, rage, anguish, loneliness, reverence, connection, and perplexity.

It's a shared adventure that everyone does on their terms.

Grief is complex and multifaceted: No two souls mourn alike, for no two losses are identical. Attempts to confine the grieving process within cookie-cutter stages, rigid criteria, and prescribed timelines propagate the fallacy of a right or wrong way to grieve.

Grief, in its essence, is a natural phenomenon—

A sacred dance that unfolds within the depths of our being. It is a deeply personal and profound experience, far from being a pathological problem to be solved.

A child's heart carries the imprint of a parent's absence for months or years. Similarly, a parent's longing for a child, partner, or loved one transcends all notions of time. The ache, the longing, lives in the very essence of our human nature.

Grief is an enigmatic path; Grief isn't linear.—

If we were to create a line graph of our grief journeys, it would be surprising for scientists to discover no discernible pattern.

Within the ebb and flow of our grief, we encounter good and bad days interwoven in a twisted dance.

Embracing this is how we move with our grief. Labeling and attempting to confine it only breeds resistance. Progress lies *not* in imposing a specific timeline but in surrendering to the ever-changing flow of our grief and learning to move on with acceptance and dignity.

04

Grief isn't inherently harmful.

Grief is evidence of love lost.

It serves as a poignant symbol of our love, our desire to cherish and remember those individuals and relationships that hold deep significance in our lives.

It's instinctively human: both beautiful and painful. By labeling grief as a problem in this sacred space, By labeling grief as a problem to solve, we carry it. By leaning into our pain, we *move with* it.

05

Grief looms of isolation. Support becomes our lifeline.

Grief defies measurement, transcending the confines of milestones as the 5 Stages of Grief imply. It is an ever-evolving journey, an ongoing experience. Pathologizing and diagnosing grief makes it feel abnormal. In reality, it represents so much of the human experience.

Diagnoses can empower us by illuminating how our minds or bodies function differently and offering solutions. However, diagnosing grief only deepens the shame, loneliness, and isolation. No one should feel wrong for grieving beyond a specific date.

We need grief support, not grief diagnosis. By creating space for its expression, allowing its capacity to unfold without restraint.

Unlock the Profound Power of Healing with EMBRACE

The 7 Stages of Grief Alignment

Are you prepared to immerse yourself on a journey of healing and self-discovery?

Step into a sphere of authenticity, truth, and love as you immerse yourself in the unparalleled wisdom and guidance offered in the transformative EMBRACE course. This course goes beyond the ordinary, offering a depth of healing that will leave an indelible impact.

What sets EMBRACE apart? It emerges from the heart of an expert grief practitioner, infused with the spirit of authenticity and infused by a genuine desire to empower and support individuals on their unique healing journeys.

EMBRACE offers a transformative approach that transcends traditional teachings.

Through this meticulously crafted course, you will unlock the tools and techniques to navigate the depths of grief, embracing healing and growth. The 7 Stages of Grief Alignment workbook becomes your trusted companion, providing compassionate guidance through each stage. It empowers you to honor your journey, embrace your emotions, and pave the way for a purposeful shift.

However, EMBRACE's path forward still needs to be completed. Those interested in learning more and becoming certified "Healing it Forward" practitioners will find that this course provides a beautiful opportunity to do just that. As a trained professional, you will be honored to assist others on their journey to wholeness and personal development.

The EMBRACE program is an astonishing journey of self-discovery and empowerment, not simply another healing class. It encourages you to look within, where you'll find the key to your inner wisdom and the key to your recovery. Along the journey, you'll be surrounded and transformed by a community of like-minded spirits who share your unyielding dedication to growth and give support and encouragement.

Are you prepared to take your life's most incredible life-changing healing journey? Join us on this life-altering adventure, where our north stars are sincerity, honesty, and love. Learn the true meaning of pivoting with intent through your experience with EMBRACE. Your healing journey awaits, and we are here to walk alongside you every step of the way.

Are You Ready?

ALL RIGHT, GRIEF WARRIORS:

We're breaking up with the 5 Stages of Grief

Meet your new boo,
the 7 Stages of Grief Alignment!

The 7 Stages of Grief Alignment knows no order. They are not
steps but continual pillars, symbols, and actions to make
space for grief in your growth.

*Words hold immense power, and we choose to
transform our grief rather than diagnose it.*

The Grief Warrior

EMBRACE

THE 7 STAGES OF GRIEF ALIGNMENT

01

EXPRESS
Let your emotions guide you and experience the joy and fulfillment of expressing your true self through journaling and artistic exploration.

02

MEDITATE
Embrace the power of sitting with your grief, opening your heart, and leaning into the serenity of the present moment, creating space for healing and growth.

03

BE PRESENT
Pause. Observe and relinquish the need for constant busyness, and tune into the depths of your feelings. Embrace the beauty, opportunity, and purpose in this moment.

04

REJUVENATE
Reignite your zest for life, nourish your soul, and elevate your vibrations through the transformative power of self-care. Rediscover what it means to feel truly alive.

05

AWAKEN
Awaken the part of you that's been hiding. Reclaiming lost joy, energy, and vibrance. Rediscover the essence of your true self, waiting to be revealed.

06

CONNECT
Grief can separate us from true ourselves, making us feel like trapped observers of our lives. Reconnect physically, mentally, and spiritually to find your center and regain a sense of control and profound connection.

07

EAT HEALTHY
Nourish your body with the fuel it craves for strength and vitality. Embrace the sensory delight of flavors, textures, and intuitive connection as your body receives each healthy bite.

What 'stage' speaks to you?

IF YOU'RE READY TO TURN YOUR PAIN INTO FUEL...

Your past can lead you to your purpose.

Your pain can become your fuel to embody and fulfill that purpose. It's time to heal the resilient spirit within you, the one who has overcome more than imagined possible.

Unclench your jaw. Let out a sigh of relief - and stop running. We can't change our pasts. e may not alter our pasts, but we can find peace in our history and shape our futures by nurturing our souls in the present moment.

Each of us possesses a unique narrative shaped by our experiences. While we may not always have control over the plot, we have the power to choose the underlying theme. Let us craft our stories around the essence of healing rather than being defined by pain.

Rise as a warrior, not just a survivor. I am here to guide you because I believe in your strength.

It's time to take hold of the reins and chart a path toward healing, love, and inner strength.

Your past paves the path to purpose.

i believe in you.

Grab a pen, and we'll embark on your new journey together.

PIVOT *with* PURPOSE

My vocation is a sacred calling, where every word, line, and page is carefully crafted with intention and purpose. My vocation extends far beyond the conventional realms. It transcends the boundaries of traditional academia and ventures into the realm of energy and transcendence.

Having traversed the depths of deep trauma and loss, I intimately understand the weight of grief and despair. Yet, I alchemize that suffering into meaning through the art of writing, creating, and teaching. I am fueled by authentic and intentional love in every breath of my life.

It is not a love born out of obligation but a love that empowers and inspires, beckoning others to rise above their fears and embrace the limitless possibilities that lie within them.

To me, this is the very essence of sacredness.

Let this inspire you that, no matter your challenges, you can *Pivot with Purpose* and manifest life in alignment with your highest energy. As your Grief Warrior® mentor, I will guide you on a sacred transformation journey.

The Grief Warrior

I HAD TWO CHOICES:
Retreat Or Renew

When my first-born son passed away, grief consumed me. I could have withdrawn from life, but a fire within me refused to give up. It was then that I realized grief is the expression of love. It's our mind and heart's way of grappling with loss. It requires embracing the unknown, for life itself is unpredictable, regardless of our beliefs.

In rediscovering the magic of life, I rekindled my commitment to live truly. The grief didn't vanish, but it became more manageable. I started noticing the small things that bring joy to life. Each day became an adventure filled with endless possibilities. With an open heart, I welcomed the uncertainties that came my way. While the aftermath of a loss can leave us feeling hopeless, the strength to persevere can lead to unexpected achievements. Withdrawing may seem tempting, but it only perpetuates a downward spiral. We can move forward and rediscover joy by renewing our commitment to purposeful living.

I crafted the 7 Stages of Grief Alignment to renew my commitment—a guide from eleven years of personal experience and introspection. My book, A Son's Gift, became a testament to living intentionally after unforeseen circumstances. This challenge navigates the unexpected tragedies that may befall us, particularly if we face intense grief for the first time. Each stage holds significance, and we must traverse them daily. It isn't always easy, but a life infused with meaning and purpose is worthwhile.

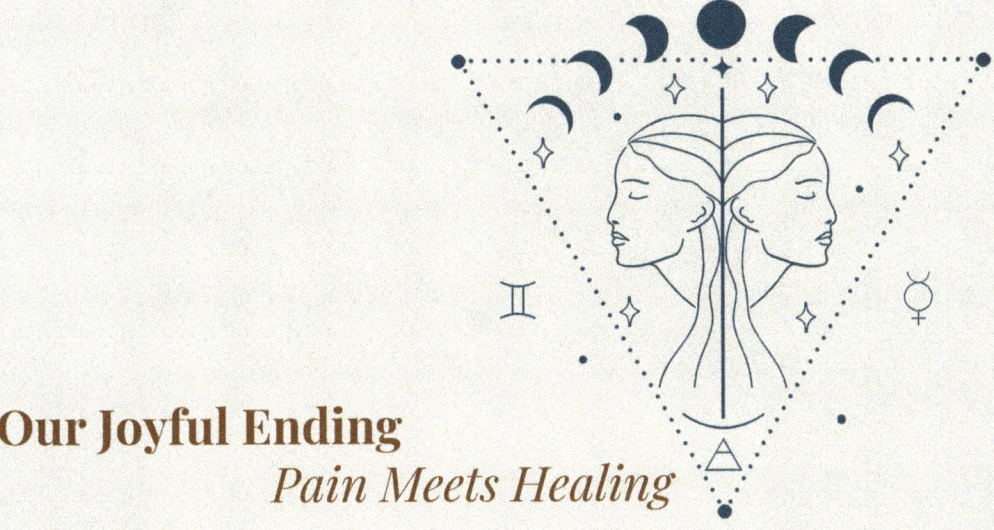

Our Joyful Ending
Pain Meets Healing

Once upon a time,

...in the whimsical land of Serenityville, a group of courageous warriors known as the Serene Seekers set forth on a remarkable quest—the Journey of Healing it Forward. Guided by the wise and enchanting fairy Seraphina, they discovered the secret power of acceptance. The goal was to align with the 7 Stages of Grief and release the mystical power inside.

The Serene Seekers set out on their journey full of bravery and love. As they wandered through enchanted forests and sparkling waterways, they experienced times of hardship. They didn't shy away since they knew the answer to their problems resided within themselves.

The Serene Seekers blazed a trail based on the ancient wisdom of the 7 Stages of Grief Alignment. Each phase—"Express," "Meditate," "Be Present," "Rejuvenate," "Awaken," "Connect," and "Eat Healthy"—held a vital piece of the puzzle to their recovery and development.

Under Seraphina's guidance, the Serene Seekers learned that pain was not their enemy but a teacher to be embraced. It became a part of their story, a testament to their courage and resilience. United in their journey, they supported one another, sharing stories and offering solace when needed. Their empathy and compassion wove a love web across Serenityville.

By embracing their pain, the Serene Seekers discovered the profound magic of healing it forward. They realized their healing could inspire and uplift others, spreading hope and resilience far and wide.

The Serene Seekers' journey through the 7 Stages of Grief Alignment showcased the power of acceptance and showed the world how beautiful it can be. Their travels exemplified the concept of "healing it forward," the idea that one person's kindness may positively impact others.

And so, the Serene Seekers continued their noble quest, fueled by determination and love. Together, they embarked on the Journey of Healing It Forward, embracing their pain, sharing their stories, and spreading seeds of healing throughout Serenityville and beyond.

This uplifting tale illustrates the power of facing our suffering and moving with "Healing it Forward."

HOW TO
Sit *with* Your Grief

ACKNOWLEDGE IT.

OWN IT.

EXPLORE IT.

THERE ARE *3*

FUNDAMENTAL

STEPS TO EMBRACING YOUR GRIEF

FEEL *and*
ACKNOWLEDGE IT

Feel - Dive into the Depths of Emotion In the first step. We will learn the art of feeling. Relax your body and mind by closing your eyes and taking a few slow, deep breaths. Don't oppose or judge the feelings you're experiencing.

Are you on the verge of purging, overwhelmed by a storm of pain, guilt, shame, betrayal, or envy?

In EMBRACE, you will understand the depth of your pain through emotional exploration. Embracing our feelings shows respect for the integrity of our experience and lays the foundation for healing.

To *acknowledge* is to embrace the power of acceptance with the courage to feel. It is easy to dismiss our grief, burying it beneath layers of denial or self-judgment. But this step teaches us to embrace our pain by acknowledging its presence. Let go of the urge to push your feelings aside or berate yourself for struggling. Instead, recognize that grief is a natural and valid experience. When you own your suffering, you allow yourself the time and perspective to determine what's causing it.

OWN YOUR FEELINGS
of Pain, Grieving, Loss

Understanding your feelings is the first step, but owning your pain is crucial. Grief is often associated with a side of ourselves that we prefer to ignore, so we dismiss it. However, pushing your emotions aside or criticizing yourself for struggling can worsen things. Instead, it's essential to accept your pain as a natural and valid experience and take responsibility for it.

By holding yourself accountable, you can create the space and understanding necessary to delve deeper into the issue and uncover its root cause. This process of self-exploration allows you to work with your pain rather than fighting against it, leading to gradual healing and release from its grasp. With time, you may find that your pain becomes a source of wisdom and inspiration, helping you cultivate self-compassion, acceptance, and strength.

So, don't dismiss your pain or judge yourself for feeling it. Embrace it as an opportunity for self-discovery and growth, and let it guide you on your journey.

ARE YOU LIVING A LIFE *of Denial?*

Denial is a tempting refuge, an escape from facing the truth that awaits us. But is it truly living?

Yet, in denying our true selves, we rob life of its vibrant colors. We become sleepwalkers, traversing existence without truly seeing or experiencing its wonders. Disconnected from our emotions, we numb ourselves to the essence of our being, avoiding the aspects of life we dare not confront.

Grief has a way of leaving us feeling empty, disconnected from the world. Faced with such turbulent emotions, it is crucial to remain present. Opening ourselves to the surrounding reality allows us to reestablish our connection to ourselves and the world surrounding us.

If denial has become your shield for too long, it is time to confront the truth. Though it may be a painful pilgrimage, evading your emotions and sidestepping the obstacles that impede your growth will only perpetuate your suffering. To live a life of integrity and authenticity, we must be brave enough to acknowledge our wounds and fears.

Embrace the journey, for it may come with its share of challenges. Remember, transformation is not an overnight process; it requires time and intense dedication. But as you courageously confront your pain, you will uncover hidden wells of strength within. Say goodbye to denial and welcome the truth of your existence. With each intentional step, you carve a path toward a life filled with authenticity and purpose.

The path ahead may be arduous, but you are not alone. I am here to offer my unwavering support, accompanying you through every stride of this transformative journey. Embrace your inner resilience and have faith in the healing process.

Trust yourself and step boldly into a life of authenticity and growth. You have the power to rewrite your story.

The Guiding Light of *Embrace* Nurturing Those in Grief

Faced with another's grief, we often find ourselves at a loss for words. The profound pain and sorrow they bear can leave us powerless, uncertain of how to offer solace in their darkest hours. Yet, amidst the vastness of this challenge, there exists a flare of hope—a well-crafted grief book, EMBRACE.

In these pages, you'll find a companion journal that will bring comfort and understanding to those roaming the twisted path of sorrow.

While it is impossible to erase the pain, EMBRACE can soothe the aching heart and guide one's steps through the obstacles of grief.

The sentimental narratives make the emotions' kaleidoscope more explicit and the burden of grief more tolerable. As a treasured tool in your grief bag, the 7 Stages of Grief Alignment provides a roadmap for the griever and their companions, fostering awareness and healing.

Yet, it is crucial to remember that when supporting someone living in grief, the gift of your presence and enduring willingness to listen outweighs any words of wisdom or reassurance.

With its intricate nuances, grief often leaves those who mourn feeling isolated and misunderstood. EMBRACE is a heartfelt promise that assures you that you are not alone in your journey.

EMBRACE will offer hope and encouragement, reminding readers they are not alone in their sorrow. Consider giving them a copy to support a friend or loved one during grief.

If you want to support a friend or loved one during grief, consider giving them a copy of EMBRACE! You want the support of your loved ones, and the same goes for them needing you. As with any journey in life, the journey of grief as a team, we got this!

The Healing Dance of Grief
Nurturing the Spirit *within*

When someone close to us dies tragically, we are engulfed by an overwhelming sense of loss, accompanied by a symphony of painful emotions. We journey through this dimension of grief, uniquely navigating its twists and turns. Some shed tears like raindrops from a stormy sky, others ignite with fiery anger, while some retreat into the solitude of their inner world. These reactions, these expressions of grief, are the rivers that flow from the depths of our souls. We must honor them, for within these expressions lie the seeds of self-awareness and the catalysts for healing.

It's simple to feel disoriented and overwhelmed in today's fast-paced, ever-evolving society. The grieving process is a multifaceted test; we all long for the loving company of a compassionate that requires us to seek comfort from those who can relate. As a holistic practitioner, I stand ready with the tools and resources to accompany you on this sacred pilgrimage. Drawing upon my extensive experience, I offer a sanctuary where your voice can be heard, your story shared, and your healing ignited.

Discerning the way forward is exhausting in life's chaotic orchestra, where confusion and uncertainty reign. The weight of emotional pain may tempt us to forge ahead, mindlessly seeking an escape from the obstacles that hinder our progress. Yet, dear soul, a profound wellspring of resilience and strength lies within you. Developing spiritual growth can lead to a limitless abundance of peace and stability. Nurturing your connection with a higher power or the wisdom within you can help you navigate life's most brutal storms with grace and serenity. As you enter this sacred journey of spiritual expansion, you will uncover newfound capacities to navigate life's turbulent seas, supporting your passage and extending a loving hand to those who traverse similar paths.

The road may appear dimly lit as you tread its winding path. Yet, within you resides a radiance of faith, highlighting the darkness for those who desire comfort in your presence. Even when grief looms, keep hope alive in the sanctuary of your heart. I encourage optimism even in the darkness. Envision a shining star, your inner strength shining its light into the deepest crevices of despair. As you gaze upon the darkness, challenge fear and vulnerability to manifest and transform into a conduit for healing. By embracing the full spectrum of your being, shadows, and all, you control the destiny of self-empowerment. Even in the trenches of darkness, your intense light inspires and uplifts those who witness your strength and courage.

Remember that you are never alone in the sacred dance of grief, where each step is steeped with the essence of unconditional love. Reach out, Warrior, to those who can guide and support you on this transformative pilgrimage. Together, you will honor the pain, nurture your spirit, and spin a tapestry of healing that extends far beyond the realms of grief. Let the rhythm of your heart guide you, as it holds within it the tune of perseverance, the harmony of optimism, and the assurance of rejuvenation.

Shadows become tools that help shape Who You Are...

The Symphony of *Empathy* Navigating Responses to *Grief*

Why do some people run when I embrace my sadness?

Have you ever felt alone in your sadness because others choose to ignore or withdraw from you?

It's disheartening to question whether you deserve support or understanding. It can be challenging for those not accustomed to dealing with intense emotions like grief to face their feelings. Fear, unfamiliarity, and a lack of knowledge about responding supportively could all contribute to their feelings.

It can feel like others are trying to hide from the truth of your experience and being when they avoid hearing about your sorrowful tale. It might make you feel invisible, alone, and desperate for approval. An essential part of the grieving process is vulnerability, which searches for comfort in human connection and comprehension.

However, it is essential to note that only some can face and hold space for strong emotions, especially if they have not experienced something comparable. Their insecurity stems from a need for more ease with showing emotion. It's important not to take their reaction personally; instead, give yourself time and space to work through your feelings.

Be gentle with yourself and embrace the understanding that not everyone will comprehend or offer enduring support on this path. With time, you'll meet people who can hold the sacred space for your grief, opening doors to vital life lessons and opportunities for new relationships.

There can be many reasons why people don't respond to your melancholy expressions. Some people may struggle with displays of intense emotion, while others may feel ill-equipped to respond to someone who is deeply sorrowful. In certain instances, people may even fear that witnessing your sadness will awaken their dormant pain. It is essential to acknowledge that each person uniquely navigates grief, and adverse reactions to your sorrow do not show a lack of care or concern. Give them breathing room to deal with their feelings; they may discover the strength to help you.

As you continue your grief journey, remember that your emotions are valid and that your need for support is real. Seek solace in those who can hold space for your grief, and let go of the notion that everyone will understand. The dance of empathy requires patience and calls for self-compassion. If you care for yourself during this process, you show others how accepting melancholy can strengthen the spirit.

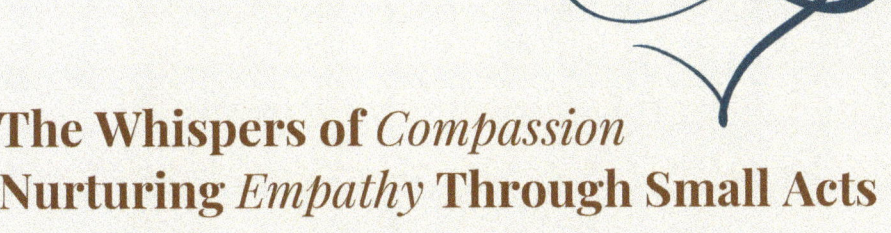

The Whispers of *Compassion*
Nurturing *Empathy* Through Small Acts

Empathy's complex webs of connection strengthen relationships during the grieving process. A kind touch, reassuring words, and a listening ear can go a long way toward alleviating emotional pain. During sadness, expressions of sympathy transform into a beautiful melody of support, kindness, and concern.

Even the tiniest gestures can convey the magnitude of affection and concern in moments of quiet reflection. Sincerity and love injected into the most straightforward actions can illuminate the darkest places. These seemingly insignificant acts go beyond words to bring solace to the soul. By doing these nice things for them, we can let them know they have our undying support and are not alone.

Sometimes, the answer lies not in words but in the silent embrace of companionship. To stand beside someone in their darkest hours to honor their wishes can transcend an act of compassion. You become a sanctuary of support for their wounded soul. Becoming a lifeline amidst the chaos by offering practical help, running errands, and preparing nourishing meals demonstrates that our warmth extends beyond mere words to sacred stillness.

They provide a sympathetic ear that accepts their suffering without judgment or making demands. We become instruments of compassion and wisdom, holding the door open for their recovery.

When words fail, being there and knowing how grateful we are can help comfort a broken spirit. Therefore, let us recognize the significance of greeting cards, reassuring embraces, and quiet moments of reflection. Aim to personify empathy, compassion, and concern. We become the vessels through which comfort is delivered, mending the broken parts of a mourning person's spirit in those quiet times.

You can use the following phrases:

My heart goes out to you; I'm sorry this is happening to you.
"What is your loved one's name?"
"What do you say we get some lunch together? Please tell me more about (insert name of cherished one here)."

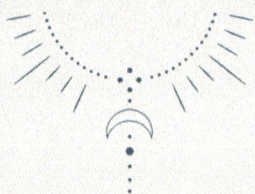

The Unseen Language of Sorrow
Embracing *Understanding* and *Letting Go*

It's frustrating when those close to you don't understand how much your loss means to you. Some wonder if avoiding those who can't share our sorrow is right. But let's PAUSE to think about this:

No matter how well you articulate your pain, not everyone can comprehend complex emotions. Despite our efforts to articulate our pain, some may struggle to grasp its true essence. In these situations, letting go of our dependence on their comprehension is not a sign of a lack of strength or inability. Our efforts to help them understand the inexplicable would be well-spent.

Don't you think it's wonderful to imagine a world where empathy is cultivated and understanding becomes a part of our collective etiquette? While that ideal may be far off, we can take comfort in the company of those who share our values and offer proper understanding and support. Seek comfort in knowing you are not alone on your grief journey. By doing so, we create space for our healing, allowing our sorrow to unfold in its way, guided by our resilience and the support of those who truly understand.

01 Let us find comfort in the arms of those who truly understand and share our pain on this developing path of sorrow. Even if others can't understand our pain, it's reassuring that some would listen with empathy and provide a safe place to heal.

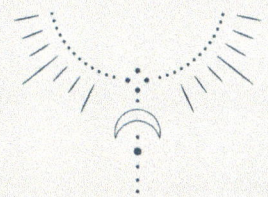

02

In the depths of sorrow, we are faced with a "griefosophical" lesson:

We are the chosen ones entrusted with the sacred duty of carrying the unseen language of sorrow. It is not a burden to bear but a calling that sets us apart from others. Our connection with our departed loved one runs deep, transcending the comprehension of others. The love we shared with them was unique, profound, and intimate, coloring our grief in hues that may mystify those who did not experience the same depth of connection.

Rather than harboring resentment or seeking understanding from those who cannot offer it, we can shift our perspective. It helps to think of ourselves as spiritual vessels that have solemnly promised to bear the burden of our grief. To mourn together is to witness the strength of love and reveal the depth of our connection.

By letting go of the expectation that everyone will understand our grief, we unlock a sense of communal understanding only discernible by our innermost beings. We become a collective source of higher consciousness. Our common grief language helps us bond with those who resonate with our vibe.

So, Warriors, Let up, hoping other people share your pain with you. Embrace the idea that you are connected to a group of people who "get it," and you become a force that cannot be stopped together. Make use of your suffering as a starting point for introspection and growth.

In doing so, you give tribute to the unconditional love you shared with your departed loved one and become that twinkle who walks this path of grief.

In grief, we are chosen to carry
the unseen language of sorrow,
a testament to our love and
resilience.

Unveiling the Art of Respecting *Grief*

In this era of digital connectivity, we find ourselves conditioned to swiftly move on and brush aside the depths of our grief. Glossing over the importance of grieving and grief acceptance might be easy in today's fast-paced world. However, grief encompasses far more than prolonged sadness; it is an emotional journey that demands time, reverence, empathy, and patience to mend.

Loss, especially the irreparable loss of love, is at the heart of mourning. When we suffer a profound loss, it changes who we are and shines a light on what gives our lives true purpose. The path to recovery and growth lies in sincerely accepting our suffering.

Nobody enjoys being hurt, and most people will try to avoid it. However, suffering is a part of being human and must be faced head-on. Grief and loss, and the emotional sorrow they cause, are experiences all humans share at some point. Neither can we expect anybody else to take away our suffering, but we can show compassion, which can teach us a great deal about how to deal with the misery of others. Through compassion, we see that the suffering of others is natural and merits our whole attention.

The ability to empathize with others serves as a helpful reminder that there is no single "correct" way to deal with suffering. It is unnecessary to have all the solutions to be compassionate; all we need to do is be there for people when they are suffering.

So, when we see a loved one going through a tough time, let's not rush to ease their suffering. Instead, let's give our undivided attention to becoming wise. By doing so, we show them the kindness and consideration they deserve. There is an act of tremendous bravery, tenacity, and grit at the heart of mourning, an act that teaches profound truths about what it is to be human. So, let's not rush past the remembrances of limitless, unconditional LOVE.

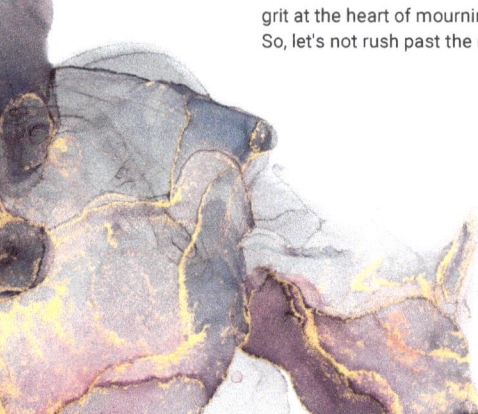

Embracing the *Everlasting* **Journey**

BOTTOM *line*

One of life's greatest challenges is coming to terms with the fact that mourning is never really "done." We may reach a point where the raw pain of our loss has begun to fade, but the scars remain. These scars can be a source of strength and comfort. They remind us of the loved ones we have lost and help us appreciate life's fragility.

But keep in mind that you will never fully "get over" your loss. It is an ongoing journey that we all must travel. There may be days when the path is smooth and the going is rough. But eventually, we will reach our destination: a place where we can find peace and happiness again.

Healing is an ever-unfolding journey, an intricate dance of self-discovery and growth. As we set out on our journey, we recognize that our wounds are not who we are but a testament to our capacity to love fiercely and persevere through adversity. Unconditional self-love feeds the soul and opens the door to healing on all levels. Putting aside baggage and focusing on what brings us joy might help us find inner freedom.

You may find that your relationship with your loved one changes as you move through grief. Their presence becomes a source of strength and comfort, reminding you of their eternal love. You gradually rebuild your life as you heal, carrying their memory within you. Their spirit entwines with yours, illuminating the path to a meaningful existence.

While healing may never be complete, grief can propel you toward a more positive emotional journey. Embracing and expressing your grief healthily allows for soul healing to begin.

express

meditate

be present

rejuvenate

awaken

connect

eat healthy

EMBRACE

DOES EMBRACE
Speak to You?

Explore the transformative power of The 7 Stages of GRIEF Alignment workbook journal, designed to support you authentically and effectively on your grief journey. Each stage of this journal is carefully crafted to nurture your physical and mental well-being, empowering you to strengthen critical aspects of your health as you navigate through the aftermath of a traumatic event. Embracing these stages will lead you to greater strength, resilience, and a revitalized sense of purpose.

Drawing from personal experiences of loss and trauma, I created the 7 Stages of GRIEF Alignment mini journal to assist those willing to EMBRACE in their healing process. Within its pages, you'll discover practices that have deeply impacted my grief journey, enabling me to navigate through the pain and embrace genuine growth mindfully. These practices have brought about timeless healing, from releasing old attachments to rebuilding a lost sense of unconditional love.

This eternal healing perfectly captures the beauty of "Healing."

Whether at the beginning of your grief journey or making progress, embracing the stages outlined in this journal can ease the burden and infuse joy into your life. Let's say you've had enough and are ready to start living again. Please join me on the 7 Stages of the GRIEF Alignment workbook journal's transformational journey, or go even further and earn your Certified Wellness Warrior designation.

Take a deep breath, stay resilient, and remember that even in the darkest moments, we possess the inner strength to move forward. Embrace this opportunity and witness its profound impact on your life. Not doing so would be a mistake.

EXPRESS

Welcome to the First Stage of Grief Alignment: Express. In this stage, we encourage you to unleash your thoughts, feelings, and trauma through emotional journaling. By embracing this practice, you voice your emotions and release anxiety, triggers, and pain.

Reflect on its meaning in your grief journey and explore its significance. Use your notebook as a place of refuge where you may explore who you are and how you got here. Allow your own words to heal and shape your spirit.

Three ways you can integrate 'Express' into your daily therapy:

Emotional Journaling
Write freely each day to express and process your emotions.

Artistic Expression
Engage in creative activities to communicate and release emotions.

Verbal Communication
Share your feelings with a trusted person or practitioner for support and validation.

Expression is the key to unlocking our connection, allowing us to co-create a reality rooted in love and acceptance. So say their name, share your story, feel every moment, and remember—you are here for a reason. And always remember—you are here with a purpose. You have the power to create. So keep expressing yourself—you have everything it takes to thrive!

How will you express today?

MEDITATE

Have you ever explored the richness of meditation? It offers a gateway to discovering tranquility and clarity in grief or challenging moments. By dedicating time to cultivating mindful awareness, we unlock the potential for remarkable revelations.
With each intentional inhalation and exhalation, we create a sacred space within ourselves, allowing us to confront our emotions from a higher perspective.

Discover peace in nature's embrace, where meditation unveils transformative insights.

Pause for a moment and ask yourself: When was the last time you truly paused and immersed yourself in the vivid reality of "here"? It is in the here and now, the ever-present moment, where true existence lives. It is within this moment that the miracle of life unfolds.

BE PRESENT

'Be Present' is the 3rd Stage of Grief Alignment, encouraging us to be still. Society often expects us to conform to specific standards, but we have the power to within ourselves begin a path toward wellness simply by showing up.

Being present allows us to reconnect with life, love, and feel again.

Let's focus on being present and mindful. Pay attention to your breath - feel the rise and fall of your chest and let it move like a symphony's crescendo. Focus on the present and feel the caress of each inhale and exhale. Take in the vibrant feelings that sweep your entire being, and let them merge with the present moment.

Allowing your emotions to take over can be liberating. Accepting and working with our feelings without hesitation or judgment is crucial. Whatever those emotions may be, it's okay to feel them. Take a moment to permit yourself to step back, allowing your soul to have time within this very breath.

REJUVENATE

For true revitalization, we must turn inward and examine our bodily, mental, and spiritual states.

It can help us reclaim our vitality and lead us toward joy and fulfillment, especially when dealing with the loss of a loved one or the constant stresses of modern life. Transformation comes with self-reflection, inner growth, and healing. You have the power to do this!

By embracing new challenges and striving to grow in every aspect of our lives, we can reignite the spark and fire up our souls. So, why wait? We can rejuvenate and awaken joy at every level with determination and self-acceptance.

Reflecting on our loved ones and the gifts they gave us can also help rejuvenate our lives in their honor. Whether remembering a favorite memory or reaching out to those who supported us during difficult times, each act deepens the connection between us and our loved ones, even as they move beyond the physical world.

Ultimately, we choose how to react to grief, but by acknowledging our journey and embracing joy, we can find strength in our spirit again.

AWAKEN

In the 5th Stage of Grief Alignment, Awaken, you are invited to embrace the essence of being fully alive and anchored in the present moment. Retaining and shielding ourselves from raw emotions and harsh realities is expected in the depths of grief.

Awakening is the key that unlocks the door to our inner resilience and rekindles our faith in the truth that lies before us.

Pause and contemplate your life as it stands today. Allow this fresh perspective to offer a broader view, enabling you to observe your journey from a distance. In this introspection, you may realize that all you need lives within, and a vast expanse of possibilities awaits you on the horizon.

Let's embrace the awakening, as it acts as a catalyst that propels us forward with a renewed sense of vitality and purpose on our journey.

CONNECT

In the 'C' of EMBRACE, we find the power of connection in the 6th Stage of Grief. As we make our way through the complexities of this world, now is the moment to strengthen our connection to ourselves, our spirit, and our mind. While it may pose challenges, remember that we all thrive on daily connections.

How will you choose to CONNECT today?

Your mind. Your body. Your spirit.

Make a conscious effort to connect with yourself by dedicating just five minutes to express gratitude, a walk in nature, engaging in reflective journaling, cooking, creating, or allowing yourself to be still. Focus on self-care and self-reflection to enhance your well-being.

Tune in to your needs and honor them, for it is in these connections that true healing and growth can flourish.

EAT HEALTHY

In the final stage of our grief alignment journey, we are called to embrace the importance of nourishing ourselves through healthy eating. As we have journeyed through the different stages of grief in our course, we have learned the significance of addressing our emotional, mental, and spiritual needs. Now, we focus on the physical aspect of our well-being, recognizing that what we put into our bodies directly impacts our healing process.

Eating healthy becomes the inner thread that weaves all the stages of our grief alignment journey. By nourishing ourselves with wholesome, nutrient-rich foods, we provide our bodies with the fuel to support our healing from the inside out. We actively participate in our healing process by prioritizing foods promoting strength, vitality, and well-being.

As we continue our journey beyond grief, let us carry healthy eating lessons. Let us embrace the power of wholesome foods to support our ongoing healing and growth.

It is through this holistic approach that we can truly thrive and create a life that is vibrant, nourished, and filled with joy.

YOUR INNER
spiritual warrior!

EMBRACE is the ultimate exhilarating journey of healing and transformation. This course is not just a certification—it is a profound commitment to healing and a powerful dedication to moving forward with purpose.

We encounter countless challenges that test our resilience and tempt us to give up. Yet, deep within us lies an untapped well of strength, waiting patiently to be discovered and unleashed. This course empowers you to tap into that inner strength, unlock your full potential, and become the vessel to *healing it forward*.

The key lies in listening to your heart and trusting your instincts. By tuning into the untapped wisdom at the core of your being, you gain the clarity and guidance needed to navigate any obstacle that comes your way. With a resilient focus, you cultivate the courage and determination required to **move with** emotional barriers.

As you EMBRACE this journey, you discover that nurturing your inner world positively impacts your external world, cultivating meaningful connections with others, and investing in your self-enlightenment. The key lies in listening to your heart and trusting your instincts.

The 7 Stages of Grief Alignment will be your guiding light as you EMBRACE each stage of grief in your own time. Recognize that these stages are not linear processes; you may move back and forth between them as you navigate your unique grief journey. This flexibility allows you to honor your experience and progress at your own pace.

Are you ready to step into your power as a Certified Grief Wellness Coach?
Sign up today and trust your inner calling, take that leap of faith, and let your guiding light illuminate the path of healing and transformation for yourself and others.

A Graceful Pivot to Purpose

you've made it

You are now ready to **EAT HEALTHY in** our Final Stage:

— eat healthy —

That's the blessing and power of **pivoting with purpose.**

What are the 7 Stages of Grief Alignment?
Express. **M**editate.
Be Present. **R**ejuvenate.
Awaken. **C**onnect. **E**at Healthy.

The power of embracing awaits as you stand at the cusp of this last stage of our journey chapters.

The question remains:
Are you prepared to journey onward and upward?

Table of Contents

WELCOME
Tuning into Your Body

Grand Rising, Wellness Warriors!

This final pillar of EMBRACE —
emphasizes the importance of
EATING HEALTHY

As we arrive at this pivotal moment in our EMBRACE journey, let's acknowledge the profound essence of EATING HEALTHY.

This final stride towards embracing our holistic selves is about taking decisive mental and physical steps. It's about harnessing the wisdom and strength we've accumulated thus far and putting it into daily practice. When we embrace compassion and adopt fresh perspectives, we fortify our mind, body, and spirit, enabling us to live with purpose and intention based on the insights we've garnered throughout our journey.

Treating our bodies respectfully isn't just a choice; it's a testament to understanding their value. Think of your body as a cherished home, a sacred space that requires care and attention. When we choose foods rich in nutrients, we cater to our physical well-being and sharpen our mental clarity.

As we delve deeper into EMBRACE, we must remain present and attentive. We've all been guilty of eating without truly appreciating the flavors, textures, and nourishment that our food provides. However, this guide aims to change that. Through its pages, we'll uncover the transformative power of mindful eating, turning our daily meals into moments of self-healing and gratitude.

By the end, we hope to instill an enduring appreciation for food as a source of nourishment and well-being.

I hope you enjoy every page, every word, and every taste.

With Infinite Intention,

The Grief Warrior

YOUR COMMITMENT STARTS NOW

Sacred Cleanse

It is recommended to flush once a month, ideally during a full moon.

1 Quart of Distilled Water
1 Teaspoon of Aluminum Free Baking Soda
1 Teaspoon of Sea Salt

Start this cleanse in the morning.
Mix until thoroughly mixed.
Divide into four doses in a glass.
Drink every two hours.

With Infinite Intention,

The Grief Warrior

*Suggested recommendations can be purchased on my website
*Please read the recipe disclosure before starting any kind of cleanse

LESSON 1

Gut Health 101:
Education Begins at the Kitchen Table

OBJECTIVE:
To explore the gut-brain connection and create a
healing inner sanctuary.

A NOTE OF LOVE

Trust Your Gut

Shall we discuss food?

Food serves a purpose beyond sustaining our existence. Our mealtimes dictate our social events, internal routines, and daily schedules.

But what we eat is even more central than this.

Our bodies serve as our instruments and temples, allowing us toexpress, meditate, explore, heal, and grow. The connection between our minds and bodies is direct; pain in one affects the other. When we prioritize the care of our bodies, we send a message to our souls that we are important. In doing so, we create a safe and supportive environment for our trauma to settle, process, and heal.

> "Eat in Moderation. Live in Moderation. Your Temple is What You Consume"
>
> *Michelle Bell*

It is possible to transform the mundane act of eating into a meaningful ritual that promotes healing. By dedicating time to nourish, sustain, and elevate our bodies, we can cultivate a space of acceptance and embrace.

Maintaining a healthy diet is not only beneficial to our physical appearance but also to our emotional well-being. Shedding extra weight can help us let go of past pain or stress. Altering our food choices can demonstrate our commitment to self-care and the conscious consumption of nutrients.

There is a strong connection between our bodies, minds, and souls that we often overlook. This isn't just a guide on healthy eating but a holistic approach to healing that involves physical movement, mental and spiritual well-being, and releasing internal traumas. The ultimate goal is to heal your inner sanctuary.

And it all begins in our guts.

Our gut health is the root of our overall well-being. It impacts our mood, mental health, inflammation, and immunity.

Serotonin (the 'happy neurotransmitter') is one of the essential messengers in our bodies. It helps regulate various bodily functions such as emotions, focus, behavior, sleep, digestion, healing, sex drive, blood flow, and breathing.

Did you know that nearly 90% of our body's serotonin is produced in our gut, according to research?

Did you know that 90% of our physical and mental well-being originates from what we consume through our stomachs? It's true, we truly are what we eat.

If you're feeling overwhelmed, take a deep breath. We can't control everything in life, but we can control what we eat. To take charge of your health, begin by looking after your gut.

Imagine your gut as a garden that needs some care and attention. The soil of this garden is your intestinal environment, where over 100 trillion microbial cells reside. The seeds of this garden are the beneficial bacteria that keep it healthy.

To ensure the health and growth of your garden, it is essential to provide the seeds and soil with proper nutrients. One helpful fertilizer is prebiotics, which can help reduce inflammation. Oats, bananas, lentils, asparagus, and even coffee are rich in prebiotics and can benefit your plants.

Did you know that probiotics function like the flowers in your garden? They help protect our bodies and support our immune system.

It's essential to be mindful of consuming unhealthy substances like sugars, alcohol, and caffeine, as they can be likened to weeds that can overtake our system. Allowing these substances to dominate can worsen mood disorders, depression, anxiety, and inflammation. They can also impede our growth and healing by interfering with the communication needed to manage our moods, recovery, and bodily functions.

Let's work together to cultivate this garden and establish a vibrant, flourishing, and harmonious the inner sanctuary that nurtures our healing center. We'll learn how to tend to it with care and commitment.

JOURNAL

Please respond to each prompt and take out a separate journal with a minimum of 1-3 paragraphs. Allow yourself enough time to contemplate, make meaningful connections, and become inspired.

TRUST YOUR GUT

What specific nutrients or dietary components provide power, energy, and alignment in the human body, and which foods are rich sources of these nutrients?

_____

_____

_____

_____

_____

_____

_____

What are some common dietary factors or specific foods known to potentially cause lethargy, lack of focus, or hindered performance, and how can they be avoided or minimized in a balanced diet?

_____

_____

_____

_____

_____

_____

_____

_____

JOURNAL

What are the long-term benefits of prioritizing one's body and health, and how can this mindset positively impact various aspects of life?

_____

_____

_____

_____

_____

_____

_____

What specific goals or motivations do you have for eating healthy, and how do you plan to align your intentions with your actions to maintain a consistent and fulfilling approach toward your dietary choices?

_____

_____

_____

_____

_____

_____

_____

_____

What practical strategies or mindful practices can help transform your mealtime experience from your present routine into a meaningful and enjoyable ritual that enhances your overall well-being and connection with food?

_____

_____

_____

_____

_____

_____

_____

_____

SACRED SIPS SMOOTHIE

CLEANSE YOUR GUT

To promote a healthy gut, starting with a cleanse is important. This involves removing toxins and creating a fresh foundation for optimal gut health. One effective way to do this is by incorporating the Sacred Smoothie into your morning routine three times a week. It's a delicious way to kick-start your day and support your overall health.

Cleanse Your Gut Ingredients:

- 3 tablespoons of SEA MOSS
- Sea Moss Should be blended 1st w/water 2- Frozen Bananas
- 2 cups of Wild Blueberries
- 1/2 cup Pineapple Juice or
- 1/2 cup Alkaline Water

- Two teaspoons of Spirulina
- 1/2 teaspoon of Cinnamon
- Two frozen ginger cubes
- 1/4 scoop of Barley Grass Powder
- 1/4 handful Organic Dulse Leaf
- 1/4 scoop Amla Powder

BLEND 2 MINUTES

LESSON 2

Ayurveda:
The Art Of Eating
Healthy

OBJECTIVE:
To explore the gut-brain connection and create a
healing inner sanctuary.

A NOTE OF LOVE

Health isn't just a science — it's an art.

But we aim to revolutionize this notion.

Our understanding of health shouldn't be confined to merely what we can observe and measure. True health transcends empirical evidence, embracing the nuanced interplay between physical, mental, emotional, and spiritual selves. Within this broader perspective, Ayurveda, an ancient holistic system of medicine from India, finds its rightful place.

An essential teaching of Ayurveda lies in the balance between spirituality and our human experience. It contends that our spiritual essence and day-to-day experiences aren't separate but deeply interconnected. We must foster this connection for profound contentment, health, and love. We find deeper meaning in life by nurturing our spiritual side and aligning with our higher purpose. And by respecting our human nature – taking care of our bodies and acknowledging our emotions – we align with life's natural ebb and flow. We find the blueprint for holistic well-being and deep fulfillment within this delicate balance.

The profound secret of holistic well-being lies in the dance between the tangible and intangible, between science and art. As we embrace the teachings of Ayurveda and integrate them into our lives, we don't just exist — we thrive. Every meal, every thought, every breath becomes an act of reverence, a testament to the balance of life. It beckons us to ask: Are we merely living or artfully thriving?

"It is in balancing your spirituality with your humanity that you will find immeasurable happiness, success, good health, and love."

Steve Maraboli

Within the ancient wisdom of Ayurveda lies the understanding that our wellness reflects the world around us, encompassing the five foundational elements: air, water, space, fire, and earth. When these elements intermingle, they give birth to doshas, vital energies that balance and shape our health in distinct ways:

- **Pitta dosha** (fire & water) governs our appetite, thirst, and body temperature.
- **Vata dosha** (air & space) orchestrates our movement and the harmony of our electrolytes.
- **Kapha dosha** (earth & water) fortifies our joints and physical structure.

We each possess a dominant dosha, a blueprint that reveals the specific nutrients and minerals our bodies need to maintain equilibrium.

But Ayurveda teaches us more than just the physicality of health. It reminds us that everything in the Universe, including our food, thrums with energy. These energies interlace, rise, and fall in diverse rhythms, creating a symphony of experiences.

The Ayurvedic tradition identifies three primary energy types or Gunas:

- **Sattva,** embodies pure consciousness.

Mindful, present, and nurturing, it's the essence of the 'Pause.' Sattvic foods are raw, ripe, and fresh ingredients, like plants and elements from the earth:
- Fresh fruits, vegetables, and herbs and Whole grains
- Cheese
- Nuts and seeds
- Honey

- **Rajas**, the catalyst of change.

It's a dynamic force fueling enthusiasm and passion. Rajas foods include potent ingredients such as:
- Meat and fish
- Spices
- Fresh vegetables

- **Tamas**, represents darkness, inaction, and lethargy. The right balance can provide exhalation and groundedness, but too much can cause us to feel heavy, weighed down, and slow. Avoid this sensation by finding balance in tamas foods such as:
- Refined flour
- Fried foods
- Sugary drinks and candies.
- Alcohol, Tobacco Preservatives

As you venture further into the world of Ayurvedic eating, take a moment to Pause, Observe, and Discern. Reflect on the energies you naturally align with. The goal isn't tallying our strengths and weaknesses but cultivating a harmonious dance with our food and, in turn, our essence.

That's what health truly is:

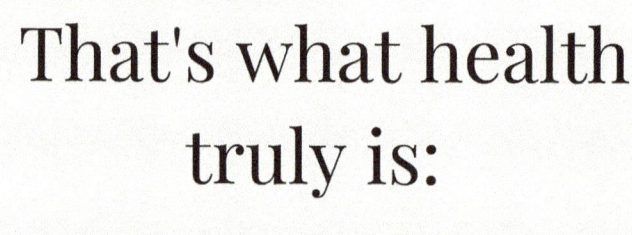

JOURNAL

Please answer each prompt while in a meditative state. Allow yourself enough time to reflect, connect, and receive inspiration. Once you have completed the prompts, you can take a Dosha quiz online.

Meeting Your Body's Inner Healer

As every dosha combines the five elements (air, water, space, fire, earth), which elements are present in your life? How might a deeper connection or balance with these elements enhance your holistic well-being?

_____

_____

_____

_____

With the understanding that everything carries energy, especially food, how might adopting a more conscious eating approach transform your physical health and mental and spiritual equilibrium?

_____

_____

_____

_____

Think of a timewhen you felt out of balance. Which dosha or guna may have been dominant then? How can this insight help you in addressing future imbalances?

_____

_____

_____

_____

_____

> *Our souls are always in transition. The more we embrace grounding in our lives,*
> *the more we tune into the PAUSE of our true alignment.*
>
> *Michele Bell*

JOURNAL

Please answer each prompt while in a meditative state. Allow yourself time to reflect, connect, and receive inspiration. Once you have completed the prompts, you may take a Dosha quiz online.

Connecting to Your Inner Sanctuary

Considering the unique energies of the doshas and gunas, which do you feel resonates most with your current state? How can understanding this dominant energy guide your path to healing and balance?

_____
_____
_____
_____

Reflecting on the foods associated with each energy type (Sattva, Rajas, Tamas), which ones do you naturally gravitate towards? How might aligning your diet with your dominant dosha foster not just physical but emotional and spiritual well-being?

_____
_____
_____
_____

Envision a future where you've harmonized with the Ayurvedic principles daily. What changes do you see in your mental, emotional, and physical health? How will this harmony influence your overall perspective on wellness and healing?

_____
_____
_____
_____

FOREST BATHING
journal prompts

Practicing writing as mindfulness can be highly helpful in preventing the build-up of overwhelming information in our minds.

Preventing us from becoming "clogged" in the channels of our mind, which over time can lead to states like brain fog, overwhelm and burnout, memory loss, insomnia, and—of course—various forms of indigestion in the gut.

Incorporating writing into your mindfulness routine can be valuable for self-discovery and growth. However, it's crucial to acknowledge the impact of the doshas on your thoughts and expression. Your constitution, current imbalances, time of day, and stage of life all play a role in determining which dosha is dominant. You can identify and work towards balancing your mental and physical elements using prompts. Before commencing with your writing practice, it's recommended to take a moment to center yourself through meditation or bodily movements. Afterward, find a peaceful spot under a tree, grab a notebook, and allow your thoughts to flow freely onto the page.

FOREST BATHING
journal prompts

VATA

Choose a body part that you feel neutral about emotionally and physically. Please write a letter to that body part and share what you appreciate about it. Set a timer for 5 to 15 minutes and only write within the limits of this creative container.

PITTA

Close your eyes and take three breaths before you sit down to write and clear the surrounding space. If you wish, light a candle or incense, or apply some essential oil or perfume to invite in a fragrance you enjoy. Open your notebook so you see two facing pages (left-hand and right-hand side), and let your writing only fill that space—stop when you fill those two pages. Write about a childhood feeling-free and playful memory, or draw or doodle any associated feelings or memories. Close your eyes and take three breaths before moving into your next activity.

KAPHA

Relocate to a comfortable spot with pillows, blankets, or a cup of tea. Set a timer for 5 to 15 minutes and jot down a list of the qualities you appreciate about yourself, your daily routine, or your present life. Keep your descriptions brief, limiting each to one line on the page. Maintain continuous writing throughout the session. Once finished, read your list aloud and select one item or activity to incorporate into your day.

JOURNAL

How have lingering thoughts or emotions clouded your mind lately? Can you pinpoint times when mental clutter led to stress or physical symptoms?

_____

_____

_____

_____

_____

_____

_____

_____

Reflect on your dosha. How do your dominant dosha's characteristics influence how you process thoughts and emotions? Have you noticed any patterns or shifts in your mental clarity or well-being when aligning with practices tailored to your dosha?

_____

_____

_____

_____

_____

_____

_____

_____

_____

SACRED SIPS SMOOTHIE

SATTVIC SMOOTHIE

To kick-start the process, let's focus on purifying your gut. This involves eliminating harmful toxins and nurturing a strong foundation for optimal gut health. One effective way to achieve this is by incorporating the Sacred Smoothie into your morning routine twice weekly.

Sattvic Smoothie Ingredients:

- 3 tablespoons of <u>Mele Moss</u>
- 1 cup Wild Blueberries 1/4 Avocado
- 1/2 cup of Frozen Mango 1/2 Frozen Kiwi
- 1/2 cup Frozen Fresh Strawberries
- 1 cup of Kale or Spinach

- 1 tsp of Cinnamon
- 1 cup Coconut Water
- 1 frozen ginger cube
- 6 Mint Leaves
- 1/4 scoop Haritaki powder
- 1 tsp Flax seed

BLEND 2 MINUTES

LESSON 3

Find the Right Diet
for You

OBJECTIVE:
Explore different diets, tune into your bodily needs,
and find foods that fuel your wellness.

A NOTE OF LOVE

Demystifying the 'Diet'

As humans, we overcomplicate things... a lot.

Dieting is an area that we have made unnecessarily complex. Our focus on health has become overly compartmentalized, compromised, and commercialized, leading to diet trends. Carbs, for instance, are deemed good one year and bad the next. Similarly, grapefruit is recommended for breakfast one year, and then bacon and eggs the next.

What's the solution? It's actually the opposite of following trends: Simplify things.

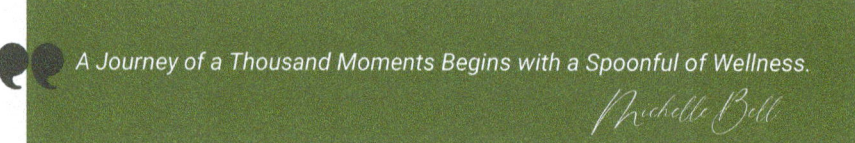

A Journey of a Thousand Moments Begins with a Spoonful of Wellness.

Michelle Bell

We can find the nutrients we need all around us on the earth. There's no need to spend a fortune on trendy diets and products when we can opt for whole foods. One such dietary approach is the Whole Food, Plant-Based (WFPB) diet, which emphasizes natural foods like fruits, vegetables, whole grains, and legumes while limiting heavily processed and animal-based ingredients.

This diet can transform our lives, backed by scientific research and ancient wisdom. It can improve our mood, energy levels, and skin, reduce inflammation, lower cholesterol, and regulate our hormones. By reducing our risk of diabetes, heart disease, and other chronic illnesses, we can achieve a more balanced and elevated state of being.

Ultimately, it all starts with our mindset and thought process.

Many of us overcomplicate dieting by believing there's only one method, one diet, and one answer for our health. But we both understand this is a misconception spread by inadequate advertising and a lack of open-mindedness.

We must learn to tune into our minds and bodies to combat it. One effective method is to identify what our bodies require by using the POD method through:

Expressing, Meditating, Being Present, Rejuvenating, Awakening, Connecting, and Eating Healthy.

When you take the time to listen to your body's cues — and give it what it needs — you initiate the healing process. You show your body that it matters. That you matter.

Throughout my wellness journey, I have discovered that gluten and dairy hinder my overall health. So, I have made it a priority to avoid them. Since implementing this change, I have noticed a significant improvement in my health, particularly after my caregiver responsibilities. My daily goal is to avoid these foods to maintain my newfound well-being.

My suggestion is always that it's all in moderation. Balance is the key to creating JOY in the journey. Find a routine that acts as a ritual for your health, reminding you to be present, tune in, and fuel your mind, body, and spiritual well-being.

Some individuals strive to discover a nutrition plan that caters to their specific body and blood type. According to naturopathic research, consuming meals corresponding to your blood type can enhance overall health and well-being by promoting greater alignment.

- Type O Blood: Eat high-protein foods, lean meats, fish, and vegetables.
- Type A: Eat plant-based, focusing on fresh, organic fruits and vegetables.
- Type B: Eat leafy greens, eggs, low-fat dairy, no gluten, nuts, corn, and seeds.
- Type AB: Eat fresh seafood, tofu, dairy, and leafy greens, avoiding caffeine.

No matter where your journey takes you, prioritize creating a harmonious and supportive environment in your gut for optimal health. Remember that your gut microbiome is vital for mental and physical well-being. It's home to trillions of microorganisms that work together to support your digestion, immune system, and mental health. Nourish it with healthy bacteria such as probiotics.

- Miso
- Kombucha
- Kimchi
- Tempeh

The abundance of super-centric food on our planet is truly a remarkable gift that can provide us with the healing properties we need.

Michele Bell

JOURNAL

Please respond to the prompts below after each meal today. This guide will serve as a reminder for you to check in with your body and listen to its needs.

Find the Right Diet for You.

What are the key benefits and long-term impacts of maintaining a healthy diet on my overall well-being and quality of life?

_____
_____
_____
_____

Considering my current eating habits, what steps can I take to enhance my overall diet and incorporate healthier choices into my daily routine?

_____
_____
_____
_____

How do you feel when you eat red meat? Sugar? Dairy? (Create a personalized menu if enrolled in the certified course.)

_____
_____
_____
_____

JOURNAL

Answer the following prompts after each meal today. Use this as a guide and reminder to check in and listen to your body:

I invite you to schedule a consultation with me to explore your options for healthy eating and discover ways to feel energized.

Do you prefer fruit or vegetables or both? Why?

_____
_____
_____
_____

How important is it for you to have a connection with your eating habits?

_____
_____
_____
_____

Write a poem expressing the significance of maintaining a healthy diet to your younger self vs. present moment.

_____
_____
_____
_____
_____
_____
_____
_____

> *Your soul is the center of your Universe.*
> *Nurturing it will nourish your inner sanctuary.*
> Michele Bell

CHOPPED MEDLEY– HEALTHY TAPAS BOWL

To maintain their distinct flavors and textures, it's best to cook barley and freekeh separately, each taking about 30 minutes. Don't worry; you can cook them ahead of time and refrigerate them for a day or two before assembling the dish. Once the grains are cooked, it's easy to put everything together. This salad is sturdy enough for a buffet table and can be covered and refrigerated for several days, but it's fluffiest when consumed within a day or two. You can serve it warm or at room temperature.

For the Salad:

- 1 cup wheat berries (or freekeh or barley)
- ¹/₂ teaspoon salt or to taste
- 1 orange
- 1 avocado
- ¹/₂ cup dates, chopped
- ¹/₂ cup figs, chopped
- ¹/₂ cup white or red grapes halved
- ¹/₂ small red onion, chopped fine
- ¹/₂ cup olives, chopped
- ¹/₂ cup pomegranate seeds
- 2 -4 red cabbage leaves
- 5 scallions or green onions, sliced thin
- 1 cup toasted pecans (or pistachios)
- 1 cup feta cheese (optional)

For the Dressing:

- ¹/₄ cup balsamic vinegar
- 1 clove garlic, minced
- 1 teaspoon manuka honey
- 1/4 teaspoon bee pollen
- ¹/₂ teaspoon dry mustard
- Sea Salt and ground pepper to taste
- ¹/₄ cup extra virgin olive oil

To prepare a delicious grain dish, fill a medium-sized saucepan with water. Next, add wheat berries and half a teaspoon of salt. Bring the mixture to a boil and let it simmer for an hour or until the grains reach an al dente consistency. Once done, drain the grains and rinse them under cold water to halt the cooking process. Transfer them to a bowl and allow them to cool completely.

Start by placing the cabbage on a flat plate and sprinkling wheat berries. Next, carefully peel the oranges and slice them between the sections before adding them to the salad. Add avocado, dates, figs, grapes, red onions, olives, pomegranate seeds, scallions, pecans, and feta cheese. Finally, drizzle some dressing over the salad, toss it all together, and serve on top of cabbage leaves.

MINDFUL EATING
tips

When it comes to our well-being, we are not just bodies with souls or souls with bodies. We must look at the body and soul together as one. There is unity between our body and soul — no matter how deeply we tune in to our spiritual practice, we also need to focus on human health-- and how we fuel our bodies. Food does not just fuel the body but the soul as well. We are this unity.

Practice taking a few moments to sit with the food before you eat it—just a few breaths to take it all in with your senses and prepare for eating.

Eat slowly, making it a point to put the silverware down after every few bites and sit back. This can take some willpower. The payoff is that as your practice of attentive eating grows, you will stop eating when you begin to feel complete. The indicator of fullness is the first belch. This signifies the stomach is letting out some air to make space for the food —so if you add more food, your stomach will run out of room. Eat slowly enough to notice the belch, and you will find it's your body's built-in system for portion control!

Try different breakfast portions over a few weeks to find the ideal amount that keeps you satiated until lunchtime, eliminating the need for snacking. Establishing a consistent mealtime routine can assist you in accomplishing this goal. It's typically more difficult to resist snacking in the afternoon than in the morning.

As you settle into a breakfast and lunch routine, paying attention to how much food you need to feel satiated until dinner is a good idea. Take note if you skip lunch and snack on sweets or coffee throughout the afternoon. To avoid this, packing a satisfying lunch can help keep you fueled and focused.

LESSON 4

The Spiritual Cleanse of Fasting

OBJECTIVE:
To explore the physical, mental, and spiritual benefits
of fasting, what it symbolizes, and how to practice it.

Reset Your Inner Rhythm

Rethinking Health and Healing: The Benefits of Fasting

Many believe the latest diet, supplements, and trendy recipes are key to our health and healing. However, fasting can effectively support personal growth, self-awareness, and spiritual development along our journey.

Fasting has physical and spiritual benefits when maintaining a healthy diet. Physically, fasting can reset the body and digestive system, allowing it to rest and heal. It can also promote fat burning, improve metabolic flexibility, and regulate insulin levels.

> *Practice discernment in moderation through faith and promise honoring our inner sanctuary. It will all come together.*
>
> *Michelle Bell*

The Spiritual Benefits of Fasting Across Different Belief Systems

Fasting is a sacred practice that has been observed in various cultures and faiths throughout human history. By detaching from material aspects and focusing on spiritual growth, fasting promotes self-discipline, mindfulness, and a stronger connection with oneself and spiritual beliefs. Let's explore how fasting is observed in different belief systems:

- In the 5th century B.C., Hippocrates recommended fasting as a healing practice.
- During Lent, several Christian denominations practice fasting.
- Many Buddhists fast daily, from noon until dawn.
- Muslims observe Ramadan, a month of fasting, prayer, and reflection.
- In Judaism, members honor Yom Kippur by fasting from sundown to sundown.
- In Hindu and Jain cultures, Ekadashi is observed twice a month, where individuals fast in sync with the lunar cycle.

Regardless of culture or belief system, fasting has been shown to provide significant spiritual benefits.

Awakening through Abstinence

Exploring the Transformative Benefits

 Increased mindfulness: Fasting requires a conscious effort to refrain from eating during specific periods. Mindfulness and self-discipline can extend beyond food and cultivate a greater awareness of one's thoughts, emotions, and actions in everyday life. It can help in breaking habitual patterns and promoting present-moment awareness.

 Heightened spiritual focus: Fasting can create a conducive environment for spiritual practices, such as meditation, prayer, or introspection. By abstaining from food, one can redirect their attention inward, fostering a deeper connection with their inner self and spiritual beliefs. This focused state can facilitate a sense of clarity, insight, and spiritual connection.

 Detachment from material desires: Fasting involves willingly letting go of physical desires and attachments, including the desire for food. This practice of detachment can extend to other areas of life, helping individuals cultivate a healthier relationship with material possessions, cravings, and external dependencies. It encourages a shift towards valuing inner qualities, virtues, and spiritual growth over external gratification.

 Purification and rejuvenation: Fasting is often associated with cleansing and purifying the body. By giving the digestive system a break, the body can redirect its energy toward healing, repair, and detoxification. This physical purification can be seen as symbolic of purifying the mind, emotions, and spirit, creating space for personal growth, emotional release, and spiritual transformation.

 Heightened sensitivity and intuition: Fasting may enhance sensory perception and intuitive abilities. With a lighter body and a clearer mind, individuals may experience heightened sensitivity to their surroundings, increased intuition, and a deeper connection with their inner guidance. This can support decision-making, intuition-based practices, and greater alignment with oneself.

EMBRACE the wisdom of your body and inner guidance, approaching fasting with mindfulness, moderation, and self-care as you honor your well-being. Through the harmonious integration of practices aligned with your true self, nourish the divine connection within and continue to pivot with purpose on a profound journey of self-discovery. You Got This, Warrior!

Unlocking Transformation

Fasting holds an intimate discipline that can guide you to higher levels of consciousness and deep inner healing. Through this practice, you cultivate strength and gain control over your appetite. Combine this newfound discipline with our Be Present - Pause - Observe and Discernment journey techniques within these writings, and you'll unlock resistance.

Fasting becomes a sacred gateway to elevated states of consciousness. By consciously abstaining from food, you create space for introspection, silence, and heightened awareness. This **PAUSE** reveals a deep connection with your inner self and the divine presence within and around you. Observing the workings of your mind, emotions, and desires during fasting brings clarity and a broader perspective that transcends the ordinary.

Alongside fasting, embrace the power of **PAUSE** in each moment, and cultivating mindfulness anchors you in the present reality, freeing you from attachment to past regrets and future anxieties. Through this lifestyle, you fully immerse yourself in the beauty and richness of every experience, discovering wisdom and healing in the simplest of moments.

Discernment becomes an invaluable companion on this transformative journey. You discern choices and influences, consciously selecting what aligns with your higher self and purpose. Fasting, combined with discernment, refines desires and empowers you to make conscious choices that support your overall well-being and spiritual growth.

EMBRACE the intimate essence of fasting, allowing it to unlock the depths of your being. Combine it with mindful presence and discerning wisdom. Through this synergy, you'll re-posture your purpose-discovery journey, access higher consciousness, and experience deep inner healing. May you open your heart to the divine guidance within your "decided life."

Fasting Modalities

Intermittent Time-Restricted Fasting

As creatures of habit, we develop a natural inclination to live, work, rest, and sleep according to a specific routine. This kind of fasting involves aligning our "internal clocks". Our mealtimes are crucial in regulating this clock. When we eat late or at irregular intervals, our bodies become disoriented, making it challenging to sleep, wake up, or stay energized when required.

Aiming to consume your meals within an 8-12 hour window every day could promote a more natural rhythm for your body, ultimately enhancing your overall health and well-being.

Intermittent Calorie-Restricted Fasting

One method of fasting centers around the number of calories or energy we consume each day. With intermittent calorie restriction, you reduce your calorie intake by 50% for two days, followed by five days of normal eating. This approach offers a weekly reset, promoting bodily cleansing and mental clarity.

Periodic Fasting

This type of fasting encourages you to limit your calories for 3-5 consecutive days during the month, eating normally for the rest.

You regain more control and intention as you find what works for your body. You become more mindful of what you eat, how you feel, and how you want to feel.

SACRED SIPS SMOOTHIE

When breaking your fast, it's important to approach it with the same mindfulness level as when fasting. Begin with nourishing foods that will set a positive tone for your day. Consider alternating between the recipes provided in previous chapters three times a week.

INTENTIONAL BREAK-FAST SMOOTHIE

- 1 tbsp of SEA MOSS
- 1 tbsp of Peanut Butter
- 1 cup of Frozen Wild Blueberries
- 1 Frozen Banana
- 1/4 scoop Haritaki powder
- 1/4 tsp Cinnamon

- 1 tsp Flax Seed
- 1/4 scoop Amla powder
- 1/4 scoop Barley Grass Powder
- 1 tsp Cocoa Powder
- 1 cup Unsweetened Almond/Oat Milk

BLEND 2 MINUTES

LESSON 5

Mindful Eating:
Embrace the Present
Nourish the Soul

OBJECTIVE:
To navigate the meaning of mindful eating, its
benefits, and how to
practice it in your daily life.

A NOTE OF LOVE

Savor It All

We've all done it:

We grab a protein bar and rush out the door in the morning. We often rush through meals, unaware of what we eat —distracted by screens and obligations. But how often do we genuinely savor the act of eating?

Amidst the chaos, daily rituals serve as anchors, providing stability in an ever-changing world. And what better ritual to bring us back to the present than the one we repeat three times a day? Mindful eating is a profound practice encompassing the physical, emotional, and spiritual realms, grounding us in the here and now.

When we engage in mindful eating, we awaken our senses and rediscover the joys of the daily human experience.

It is a powerful reminder to nourish our bodies and connect with food's flavors and sensations. Even on the most challenging days, mindful eating becomes an act of self-care. Being present for our meals, listening to our body's cues, and honoring its nourishment can provide solace and comfort.

Mindful eating goes beyond a mere buzzword; it is an intentional practice. It invites us to make conscious decisions about what we eat and when. It encourages us to listen to our bodies, disregarding social expectations and time constraints. With mindful eating, we sit down and fully experience each bite and sip, tuning in to our hunger and honoring our satisfaction.

By embracing mindful eating, we nourish our soul, finding a pause moment amidst the chaos allowing ascension to consume our inner sanctuary.

Michelle Bell

THE POWER OF PAUSE

Above all, it's about taking a moment to pause. You know the Power of the Pause if you've gone through all the EMBRACE modalities with us. A Pause between each bite allows your body time and space for digestion. It will enable you to enjoy the textures and tastes. It sets the tone for intention. A Pause at mealtime can extend into the rest of your day, encouraging you to Pause and be present throughout the rest of your life.

Let this be your guide as you begin to take a Pause of Power with each meal:

Start by focusing on how you're feeling both physically and emotionally. Identify the nourishment that would benefit you the most right now.

Listen to your body. If you feel full, stop eating and save the remaining food for later. This fosters a healthier connection between your mind and body.

Savor every bite. After each bite, pay attention to your sensory experience — the flavors, aromas, and textures.

Prepare your food with intention. This could mean shopping at a farmer's market, cooking meals from scratch, or simply taking a few moments before each meal to pause and reconnect with the food in front of you.

Eat with the sole focus of nourishing yourself. Allow yourself time to eat without distractions. Turn off the TV or put away your phone.

Create rituals around meals. This could be as simple as lighting a candle before eating or setting an intention for the meal. This helps create a sense of sacredness around what is usually seen as a mundane task.

Check-in with your body. Observe how different foods make you feel, and trust yourself enough to listen to your body signals -- provide what it needs.

Mindful eating paves the way to presence. It inspires us to slow down, savor it all, and appreciate the nourishment we're receiving. It empowers our connection with ourselves, strengthening our ability to tune in and provide for our needs.

So, savor every bite — and every moment.

JOURNAL

Answer these prompts at the end of your next meal:

Savor it All

What did I eat? Describe the tastes, textures, and sensations.

_____
_____
_____
_____

How do I physically feel at this very moment?

_____
_____
_____
_____

How do I emotionally feel at this very moment

_____
_____
_____
_____
_____

JOURNAL

How might the simple act of pausing influence the quality of your meal and your day? How can you apply the Power of the Pause elsewhere in your life?

_____
_____
_____
_____
_____
_____
_____

Write a heartfelt note to your body, expressing your deep appreciation for its remarkable ability to transform your meals into sustenance and vitality.

_____
_____
_____
_____
_____
_____
_____
_____
_____

SACRED SIPS & SNACKS CHALLENGE

Today, you will create your recipe by mindfully tuning into your body and needs. Ask yourself:

- Does my body need vegetables right now? If so, which ones?
- Does my body need fruits right now? If so, which ones?
- Does my body need grains right now? If so, which ones?
- Does my body need proteins right now? If so, which ones?
- Does my body need fats right now? If so, which ones?

My Warrior Sacred Sip or Snack Recipe

_____
_____
_____
_____
_____
_____
_____
_____

Create a grocery list based on your answers, and intentionally plan meals that fuel your needs. Listen to the Eat Healthy Meditation during this exercise.

LESSON 6

EMBRACE forward

OBJECTIVE:
To combine the seven EMBRACE modalities
altogether, aligning our journey for continued healing,
growth, and grace

A NOTE OF LOVE

EMBRACING WHAT HAS, WHAT IS, & WHAT WILL BE.

Congratulations, my wellness warrior — you've arrived. Blessed be your journey.

Eat Healthy may be the final modality in the **EMBRACE** journey, but it's only the beginning.

As we close this final chapter, I want you to begin a new story. But this time? You're the author. You're the main character. You get to decide what direction you're heading.
While you may anticipate only some plot twists, conflicts, and cliffhangers ahead, you can choose your perspective. Through the lens of **EMBRACE**, you can decide to **EXPRESS** your raw emotions, explore your endless imagination, and expand your powerful authenticity.

You can soothe the scars and pains of grief through **MEDITATION**. By tapping into your inner healing abilities, you can cultivate hope, **EMBRACE** them, and find the balance between positive and negative emotions.

When you feel caught between past pain and future fear, take a moment to embrace the pause and **BE "fully" PRESENT**. Ground yourself in the peace and stillness of the current moment.

You can raise your vibrations and **REJUVENATE** your energy to embark on a new healing path. You can honor your loved ones, yourself, and your journey with rituals of self-care and self-love.

You can remind yourself of the magic of being here now and **AWAKEN** your soul's purpose. You can envision your healing, connect to your Source Energy, and reignite each breath with renewed abundance.

When you feel lost, you can find your roots and **CONNECT** with your inner child, wisdom, and joy. You can grow and evolve by releasing what no longer serves you, making peace with your pain, and strengthening your relationship with yourself.

Lastly, it's essential to prioritize **EAT HEALTHY**--nourishing your mind and body. This will give you the necessary energy to:
Express, Meditate, Be Present, Rejuvenate, Awaken, and Connect.

Pause Observe Discern

The POD modality, consisting of Pause, Observe, and Discern, offers a powerful framework to navigate your journey with intention and self-awareness.
Let's explore how each element can be incorporated into your life during this transformative process:

Pause: Taking intentional moments of pause allows you to create space for reflection. Examples of incorporating pause may include:
- Carving out dedicated time each day for quiet contemplation.
- Stepping away from the busyness of daily life.
- Prioritizing self-care practices that replenish your energy.

Observe: Cultivating the skill of observation helps you become more aware of your thoughts, emotions, and the patterns that arise during your journey.
Examples of incorporating observation into your life may include:
- Mindfully noticing your feelings as they arise without judgment or suppression, allowing yourself to experience and process them fully.
- Journaling to explore your thoughts, emotions, and any insights that arise during your grieving process.
- Paying attention to physical sensations in your body, such as tension or discomfort, and using this awareness to guide self-care and relaxation practices.
-

Discern: Discernment involves making conscious decisions based on your inner wisdom. Examples of incorporating discernment into your life may include:
- Practicing self-compassion and allowing yourself to set boundaries with activities or people that may not serve your healing process.
- Seeking support from trusted individuals, such as friends, family, or professionals, and discerning whom to share your journey with based on their empathy and understanding.
- Make choices about how to honor and remember your loved one, whether through rituals, creating a memory keepsake, or engaging in significant activities for you.

Remember, the POD modality is a guide to support you on your unique grief journey. As you incorporate Pause, Observe, and Discern, adapt and personalize these practices to align with your needs and values. Embrace the power of the POD modality as a tool for self-discovery, healing, and growth during this transformative time.

INTUITIVE PROMPTS

Embracing is more than simply accepting our circumstances. It's far more than "moving on" or "letting go." To EMBRACE is to carve out space for both the positive and negative aspects of life and everything in between. It's embracing and accepting our most profound, darkest moments with presence and patience. It's embracing and buckling up for the rollercoaster journey of grief.

Even more?

It's pivoting from this pain to find our purpose. It's turning toward our grief and giving ourselves grace. It's honoring our loss and cultivating love.

It's time to pick up your journal!

1. How will I honor the essence of EXPRESSION as I move forward?
 a. What unique ways can I give voice to my emotions, thoughts, and experiences?
 b. Why is it essential for me to authentically express myself on this journey?

2. How will I embrace the art of MEDITATION as I move forward?
 a. What practices or techniques can I explore to cultivate inner stillness and clarity?
 b. Why do I recognize the significance of creating space for peaceful reflection?

3. How will I wholeheartedly embrace the magic of BEING PRESENT as I move *with*?
 a. What mindful rituals or practices can I incorporate into my daily life?
 b. Why is it crucial for me to fully immerse myself in the beauty of each moment?

4. How will I nourish my soul and REJUVENATE as I continue?
 a. What self-care rituals bring me a sense of deep rejuvenation and renewal?
 b. Why do I recognize the importance of restoring my energy and finding balance?

5. How will I AWAKEN my inner spirit and embrace the limitless possibilities ahead?
 a. What steps can I take to awaken my passions, dreams, and potential?
 b. Why do I believe in the transformative power of embracing my true calling?

6. How will I foster CONNECTION with myself and others as I progress?
 a. What practices or actions can deepen my connections?
 b. Why should I value the power of genuine connections on this growth journey?

7. How will I prioritize the gift of EATING HEALTHY as I continue my path?
 a. What healthy choices and habits will I cultivate to honor my body and mind?
 b. What changes can I expect to see in my overall health as a result of maintaining a balanced and nutritious diet?

Embrace your intuitive power and reflect on these prompts as you ascend, weaving your unique story of growth and transformation.

i am so proud of you

Reflect on your EMBRACE journey. If you haven't yet, read all seven books and modalities of EMBRACE to align your path forward.

Use your Journal Prompt answers to create a plan and commit to EMBRACE daily, "Healing it Forward."

Moving through grief is a challenging task. From the initial shock to the following sadness and emptiness, allowing yourself to go through it all can be difficult. But embracing our feelings and being willing to move with them will eventually bring us more joy. This gives us a heartfelt chance to honor our loved ones until we embrace them again.

The 7 STAGES of GRIEF modalities recognize this challenge and provide structure and support for intentionally moving with grief. Reminding ourselves to PAUSE in reflection during times of sorrow will help us be open to experiencing peace within ourselves, allowing the grace of the grief journey to fill our hearts until we meet those we lost again someday.

SACRED DETOX BATH RECIPES

How Detox Baths Work

Ancient wisdom and modern science combine to provide a therapeutic experience. Through osmosis, hot water draws toxic energy while cooling waters pull it away from your body as you immerse yourself in four cleansing baths - making them an ideal way to enjoy both health benefits and relaxation simultaneously!

Cleansing baths help draw toxins out of the body, allowing one to safely detoxify regularly - up 2-3 times per week with no more than once daily recommended for most people.

Baking Soda Detox Baths

Immerse yourself in an invigorating and therapeutic aluminum-free baking soda bath to help address symptoms related to radiation exposure, swollen glands, sore throats, or gums. Fill your regular-sized tub with as hot water as you can tolerate and dissolve 4 cups of baking soda until completely dissolved. Enjoy a relaxing 45-minute soak, emerging from the bath feeling rejuvenated - no need to rinse off afterward! This refreshing ritual also benefits those suffering from digestive impairments, such as stomach discomfort when digesting food.

SACRED DETOX BATH RECIPES

Epsom Salts Detox Baths

Dissolve 2 cups of Epsom salts (source) in a regular-sized bath. Use more as needed if your tub is oversized. The temperature should be comfortably warm but not overly hot. Soak for at least 12 minutes and up to 20-30 minutes. Rinse and towel dry.

Did you know that the scientific name for Epsom salt is magnesium sulfate? Although magnesium and sulfur are essential nutrients, they may not be efficiently absorbed from our diet. However, soaking in Epsom salts can help solve this issue since these minerals are easily absorbed through the skin. According to the Epsom Salt Industry Council, a simple Epsom salt soak can provide various health benefits, such as improving heart and circulatory health, reducing blood pressure, relieving muscle pain, and eliminating harmful toxins from the body. Additionally, it can enhance nerve function by promoting proper regulation of electrolytes. For general health maintenance or to alleviate the discomfort of bruises and sprains, it's recommended to soak in Epsom salts 2-3 times per week. Moreover, an Epsom salt soak can also aid in detoxifying drugs that remain in the body after surgery.

Sea Salt and Baking Soda Detox Baths

Indulge in a soothing therapeutic bath that helps reduce exposure to environmental radiation, X-rays, plane flights, and airport screenings. Add a pound of sea salt or rock salt to a hot tub filled with warm water and another pound of baking soda. Immerse yourself in the relaxing soak for approximately 45 minutes until the temperature is comfortable, then towel dry without rinsing off. For optimal results, take this bath just before bedtime and enjoy a peaceful slumber after achieving a full-body state of relaxation.

SACRED DETOX
BATH RECIPES

Apple Cider Vinegar (ACV) Detox Baths

A natural way to detoxify your body, alleviate muscle aches and pains, and reduce excess uric acid levels is by taking an apple cider vinegar (ACV) bath. To do this, add 2 cups of pure ACV to a hot bath and soak for about 45 minutes. For more oversized baths, adjust the amount of ACV accordingly. Once finished, pat yourself dry and avoid showering or bathing for at least 8 hours. This simple and effective ACV bath can relieve joint pain caused by gout or arthritis and sore muscles after physical activity. Additionally, it can help combat excessive body odor.
(Recommended once a month on a full moon-releasing and letting go!)

Contraindications

Maintaining a regular detox bath routine can significantly benefit your overall well-being. However, it's essential to exercise moderation and caution when preparing your bath. It's recommended to only stick to one formula per day and avoid mixing ingredients from various recipes, as this can lead to unforeseen complications. Additionally, if you are pregnant, it's imperative to consult with your healthcare provider before starting any detox routine. Your healthcare provider can provide guidance and advice to ensure your detox bath is safe and effective. Remember, taking care of your well-being is a top priority, and with careful consideration and proper guidance, you can enjoy the many benefits of a detox bath routine.

A Message of Encouragement for Warriors on the Journey of Life

I want to express my gratitude for embracing life's unpredictable journey. This moment is a testament to your courage and resilience.

Your spirit has grown and evolved throughout this transformative journey of mind, body, and soul. Even if the changes are not immediately apparent, be aware that your energy is shifting and your mindset is reframing. Embrace this renewal and prepare yourself for the profound transformations that lie ahead.

Life is filled with unpredictable twists and turns, but let each surprise be an opportunity to embrace every experience, no matter how unexpected. Choose to create meaning. Choose to move with it, learn from it, or grow from it. Pivot with purpose.

Every morning is a blank canvas, awaiting the masterful strokes of creation. Stop looking at changes as endings but see them as new beginnings. Will you rise to today's challenge and embrace your purpose, honoring your existence?

Remember, you've got this! With infinite intentions, MiMi.

Michele C. Bell's narrative is a profound testament to resilience, the transformative power of embracing life's most profound challenges, and the depth of human compassion. Her journey, which began with the deeply personal and original work "*A Journey of Unconditional Love*," evolved into the 22-time award-winning story, "*A Son's Gift*," marking the inception of her distinguished career as an empathetic voice within the realm of grief literature.

With a Ph.D. in Philosophy and Metaphysics, Michele brings a unique blend of intuitive insight and scholarly depth to "*The 7 Stages of Grief* - **EMBRACE**." This work, unlike traditional grief literature, opens a space where healing is interwoven with personal growth and transformation, guided by Michele's own experiences, her profound journey through PTSD, and her scholarly insights. This journey has not only deepened her understanding of grief and resilience but also infused her writing with authenticity and compassion, offering solace and a transformative roadmap to those navigating the intricacies of loss.

Her innovative approach, blending the profound depths of intuitive philosophy with avant-garde grief counseling modalities, pioneers a novel paradigm in grief literature. Michele's work, transcending meticulous writing and exploration, charts a path towards transformative healing. Each stage, encapsulated within the evocative acronym **EMBRACE**, is meticulously crafted to guide the bereaved with dignity, offering nuanced understanding through the labyrinth of loss.

Beyond her literary contributions, Michele's life story—marked by resilience amidst adversity— enriches her professional narrative. From facing challenges such as bullying and domestic abuse to navigating the complexities of being a holistic real estate broker, Michele's experiences underscore her innate desire to support individuals through significant life transitions. The profound loss of her son to Ewings Sarcoma tested her resolve, catalyzing a shift towards mental health advocacy and the development of groundbreaking methodologies like the Soul Design technique and the *7 Stages of Grief* workbooks.

Michele's contributions extend to her active involvement in suicide prevention and domestic abuse programs, where her voice has become a force for change. Her purpose, whether as a holistic real estate broker, end-of-life expert, or mental health advocate, remains consistent—to support, guide, and uplift. As a member and keynote speaker for the **Daughters of Penelope**, Michele shares inspiring messages of healing, humor, and love, emphasizing the necessity of such virtues in today's world.

At 58, Michele C. Bell, The Grief Warrior®, stands as a testament to the enduring power of the human spirit, commanding respect and fostering deep, authentic connections. Her life experiences, granting her the invaluable CAT credentials of **Compassion, Authenticity, and Trust**, continue to inspire those fortunate enough to encounter her legacy..

Testimonial

The "7 Stages of Grief" series transcends traditional grief support, offering a deeply compassionate and educational journey through the terrain of loss.

As someone who has dedicated over two decades to the pursuit of educational excellence and who has held the position of Governor for the New York State Daughters of Penelope, I've been privileged to witness the transformative power of community and philanthropy in education. Michele's work is a forward-thinking movement in this realm, embodying the essence of what it means to educate and heal.

Her approach to grief education is revolutionary, combining intuitive wisdom with a structured, empathetic methodology that guides individuals through each stage of grief in the **EMBRACE** series. The workbooks in educational curriculums would mark a significant step forward in our approach to emotional and psychological well-being, providing students and educators alike with the tools to face life's adversities with resilience and understanding the importance of emotional health as the foundation of a strong, resilient community.

I am confident that its incorporation into educational systems will not only enrich our curriculum but also fortify the hearts and minds of our students for generations to come.

Professor Lainie M. Damaskos-Christou
Governor of NYS Daughters of Penelope,
National Board-Certified World Language Teacher of Spanish and Greek

DISCLAIMER

All content within the 7 Stages of Grief Alignment Workbook is original and intended solely to promote mind, body, and spirit well-being. This material does not replace the expertise or advice of a licensed mental health professional. Grief experiences are unique to each individual, and while the workbook provides supportive tools and perspectives, it does not guarantee specific outcomes. If you are experiencing intense or extreme distress, please consult a professional.

By using this course, you acknowledge and accept these terms and conditions. The 7 Stages of Grief certification program, conceived and developed by Dr. Michele Bell, offers an innovative, holistic, and empathy-driven approach to understanding and navigating grief. It is rooted in comprehensive research and deep insight into the human experience of loss and recovery.

Program Overview:
- Embracing Growth in Grief: Recognize the transformative potential within grief.
- The 7 Stages of Grief: Explore the intricate emotional journey of grief, encompassing its multifaceted seven stages.
- Pivoting with Purpose: Equip yourself with practical tools to channel grief's raw energy into purposeful action.
- Understanding the Power of Resistance: Gain insights into the obstacles resistance can pose on the healing journey and learn strategies to address and overcome it.
- Coping Modalities: Discover and apply various coping methods tailored to individual grief journeys or to assist others on this path.
- Certification: As a culmination, the program offers a certification examination to ensure a comprehensive understanding of the 7 Stages of Grief methodology.

Engage with the 7 Stages of Grief, All-In-One Master Compilation program to acquire a compassionate and informed approach to navigating the intricate labyrinth of grief, whether for personal growth or as a professional commitment.

Remember, every voice matters in bringing light to the shadows of grief. By uniting, we can raise awareness and create a world where everyone feels understood and supported during their moments of profound loss. I deeply appreciate your commitment to this cause. Please take a moment to sign the **Loss Awareness Day** petition on **Change.org**, inspired by the heartfelt endeavors of Lisa Marie Presley. Together, we can make a difference.
With heartfelt gratitude and hope,
MiMi + The Grief Warrior ®